This captivating collection is the soul of Hawai'i and Hawaiians. Every poem in Passion's book is a family member, classmate, friend, or neighbor. I cry-laughed, especially in the poems where I saw myself.

—**Kimo Armitage**, author of *The Healers*

Passion is a sensory magician, her words an incantation that manifests all that is darkness and light and broken and beautiful in Hawai'i. From drunk uncles planning a robbery, to pulling ginger in Tutu's garden, Passion's ability to mine the depths of fractional moments of time and place, living and dying, and love and regret, elevates her to the top tier of Pacific poets.

—**Robert Barclay**, author of *Meḷaḷ: A Novel of the Pacific*

With a sober and powerful voice, Christy Passion explores a life lived in Hawai'i, a life rich with cultural heritage. Honoring this world, a world of fishermen and glass floaters, old train tracks and Sand Island weekends, these poems are both raw and beautifully crafted. They are love poems, love of home, love of the father, even love of strangers in hospital beds. Passion looks unflinchingly at what is broken in this world and what, happily for all of us, remains.

—**Adele Ne Jame**, author of *The South Wind*

Forget the travel guides and lies the Tourism Authority tells you about Hawai'i. Christy Passion's collection takes us to places that upend fantasies most of us have about paradise. Her scenes are vivid and the odors are indelible—sweat and stagnant water, sweet sour and diesel, tea that will make you live forever, and ripe mangoes sold to Chinatown vendors in exchange for movie tickets. Passion's textures are unforgettable: a patient's voice that sounds like grated ginger, and the coarse sand that shapes our way. For any journey, you need both truth and trust. *Still Out of Place* offers both in great measure.

—**Theodore S. Gonzalves**, author of *The Day the Dancers Stayed: Performing in the Filipino/American Diaspora* and *Filipinos in Hawai'i*

This collection includes an unforgettable catalog of advice about island life, family, love, and home—that murmur in our hearts that follows us throughout our lives. From a father to his daughter: "Grow teeth where your heart should be." About marriage, a mother tells her child that it's labor and "We get through it tougher. Not shinier." Grief, on the other hand, is like a tartare recipe: "Best served and consumed in small pieces." And when all hope has been exhausted and trust no longer holds weight, we are reminded, once again, that "we are rocks in ruins / rocks can spark or rocks can bludgeon / listen closely daughter / choose bludgeon." Funny, moving, and, like the family in these poems, heartbreaking and fearless, *Still Out of Place* is an impressive debut.

—**R. Zamora Linmark**, author of *The Evolution of a Sigh*

Still Out of Place

poems by Christy Passion

ISBN 978-0-910043-95-3

This is issue #109 (Spring 2016) of *Bamboo Ridge, Journal of Hawai'i Literature and Arts* (ISSN 0733-0308)

Published by Bamboo Ridge Press

Printed in the United States of America

Indexed in *Humanities International Complete*

Bamboo Ridge Press is a member of the Community of Literary Magazines and Presses (CLMP).

Typesetting and design: Rowen Tabusa

Cover art: *Under a Cobalt Sky*, 2012-13, by Russell Sunabe, oil on canvas, 60"w x 60"h

Bamboo Ridge Press is a nonprofit, tax-exempt corporation formed in 1978 to foster the appreciation, understanding, and creation of literary, visual, or performing arts by, for, or about Hawai'i's people. This publication was made possible with support from the Atherton Family Foundation, the National Endowment for the Arts (NEA), and the Hawai'i State Foundation on Culture and the Arts (SFCA), through appropriations from the Legislature of the State of Hawai'i (and grants by the NEA).

Bamboo Ridge is published twice a year.
For subscription information, back issues, or a catalog, please contact:

Bamboo Ridge Press
P.O. Box 61781
Honolulu, HI 96839-1781
808.626.1481
brinfo@bambooridge.com
www.bambooridge.com

5 4 3 2 1   16 17 18 19 20

for Pop

Table of Contents

I remember the thin tin roof and big blue fishing ball
hanging by the macramé net
open electrical wires, hibachi and ocean smell.
Try catch black aʻama crab,
scream and drop them when we do.
Race to Uncle's door when pāpio is running,
I want to tie on the wiggly bait.
Everybody is Auntie, so no need be hungry—
Auntie always has food.
Mind your family, listen and say grace before dinner.

We got there too late that day, amazed
how quickly everything came down. Sand Island
after bulldozers came and crushed
metal and wood and us   scattered.
Say something to Auntie and Uncle,
look at their faces; but,
I cannot.
I can only see the bags at their feet
and my cousins crying. Every Auntie and Uncle
with bags at their feet. Most cry,
some scream, some quiet.
Dust and noise combined with HPD push   us   back,
and I don't believe Papa anymore when he says it will be ok.

Kings

While the women were in the kitchen split between
salting the pork belly and cutting the taro stems,
and the nearest kid shuttled another Primo to Uncle Frank
before being released to play, the planning gave way
to the answer—Kalihi Super Meats.
Jimmy was the first to lean in, elbows on the fold-out table.
Yes, yes, his car was out of the shop, 7:30 Sunday morning
keep the engine running, yeah, he could do that.
Norman boy was on board but kept it cool
slouched in his chair, left arm wrapped into his undershirt,
sly smile and his mother's dimples. Bobby just laughed
but his hands were steady and his knees stopped bouncing.
It took awhile to get there: three hours of shooting the shit,
two cases of beer split between four men and challenges to
each other's manhood. By the time the late afternoon heat
blurred to a cool Kapahulu evening it was agreed
that Bobby's wife, Rosina, would distract the salesclerk
while Norman Boy and Uncle Frank worked the manager.
Two grand easy maybe even three. There was no urgency
or disguise in their talk, just a repetition of ideas polished till
all were assured and shiny. The evening star was luminous
in its indigo slice of sky. The rest of the brazen stars followed
unwavering like the gaze of badass angels—
they raised their bottles up to those ancients: to their Uncles,
Fathers and Grandfathers before them and were blessed.
Exultant as the answer braved edges, their own borders shifted—
each man now a king; growing stronger, more cunning
the odds started tipping in their favor, the rules were bending
and if anyone bothered to look at the plumeria trees
lining the yard, they would have seen them tremble.

Fatherly Advice

There are no spring days here.

Night shifts, steel-toed boots, and gin
can comfort you; you will be stronger
if you make shelter in sickness

never mind the damage of words,
real power is in hunger
and the rent, two months late

grow teeth where your heart should be,
bite anything that tries to enter;
entrance comes only through the eyes and ears
if you can see it, if you can hear it, then maybe.

Hope is for children and trust has no weight

we are rocks in ruins
rocks can spark or rocks can bludgeon
listen closely daughter
choose bludgeon.

Crabbing at the Old Train Tracks

I. K. Kaya's Fishing Supplies

Smell of dust and old rain when you enter,
the filtered sunlight through the filmy windows up top
touching the bamboo poles, nylon nets, and wood trimmed
glass case filled with metallic lures and pink glitter squids
shimmering desire; everything as it always is.
I am here with Papa, his tanned arm outstretched
over the counter to Mr. Kaya's, whose face
is all numbers and books, but his knuckles
are square and his palms are calloused;
they know hard work. The tin cans stripped of their labels
(were they asparagus? maybe tomatoes?)
line the edge of the aisles filled with small lead weights
and blunt spindles. Hanging on the wall
the cotton string crabbing nets we came for
patient and plain, like Pop's gray Kangol
hanging next to the front door.
My hands run over all the different textures
carelessly I slide my feet into rubber-soled tabis;
while I half listen to the men share their truths
about fish and family. There is no need and busy here,
just a slow belonging among the Penn reels and glass floaters
centered, unopened.

II. Bait

The butchers are at home, still asleep;
the hooks for the duck and char siu empty, yet
the fish stalls are already lit, being stocked
by lean men in rubber boots carrying
soggy cardboard boxes on their shoulders
hustling in the early morning simmer.

Buckets of ice are poured onto steel tables
for the whiskered weke and wide-eyed menpachi,
each fish neatly lined up with the next
like iridescent red-bellied dominoes.
A trough of tight-lipped Manila clams
proves irresistible to touch—
Papa motions for me to hurry along
so I let them roll from my palm
back to their family, their difficulties.
He calls out to the old Chinese man
smoking at the register, counting out coins.
Asook get aku head?
 Get, you like see?

Fish heads, heads as big as mine,
with their purple red lungs trailing
like party streamers, are held up for approval—
I clap as they are tossed into our plastic bucket,
lean over them to take in the blood smell,
the torpedo shape of their platinum heads,
tiny hooked teeth just inside the border of their mouths
agape, seemingly mid-prayer, their last fish words
not known to me. Bright gloss of their gelid eyes
glinting under the fluorescent lighting
fresh like the morning star, promising.

III. Old Train Tracks

The blue Nova kicks up the dry dirt no matter
how slowly we pull in, but no one makes the effort to go as far
as the old train tracks, so we don't have to apologize.
We unload under the misplaced monkeypod tree,

lay the nets flat, untangling the string from the floaters
without much talk; each tug and twist familiar, devout
and on the best of days, it stays mostly quiet
once the nets are cast then settled into the chamoised silt layers.
Julie's tangerine bikini top flashes taut and uncompromising—
she sets up with the good beach chair a fair distance
from the bait bucket and its mob of flies.
Pop sequesters himself under the sparse shade of thorny kiawe
holding his transistor radio against his right ear and cheek.
The sticky silver knob rolls between a talk show
touting DMSO and Frank Sinatra. I keep to the middle
balancing on the last two tracks laying on the rotted wood,
click my tongue against the roof of my mouth
tasting metal in the noonday haze, waiting.
The Pacific is not beautiful here, from the land to its mouth
there is no subtle transition. Unnatural angular rocks
form the torn shoreline once heralding a red train that carried
the Queen and her entourage. It is brown here, grubbed,
a blemish of crippled waves. When I look out at her,
unending blue with white lashes blinking at the sun,
I pity these choked off inlets, still connected
but wanting to be forgotten, like widows at a bridal shower.
There is no urgency here, no desire for ascent:
Julie's *Teen Beat*, her Farrah Fawcett hair, the sound of Pop
pissing behind the Nova, his white undershirt slack,
the water from the melted ice in the Igloo flecked with dirt
and suicidal gnats as I splash it against my neck,
we are not beautiful Hawaiians here.

IV. The Pull

It's time
the only mistake now is stopping;
once the cord is touched, pull with the chest twist at the waist—
    maybe it'll be another monster like the six-pound beast
from two summers ago, pulled up right there
defiant, cutting through the net with his black striped claw

eyes on the eddy, there's the orange floater
swaying towards the gray surface, then the metal rim—
    maybe it'll be blue crabs, soft shelled, Mama's favorite,
newspaper spread out over the counter first then
the thwack of the butcher's knife splitting them in two

the water's letting go, hands keep gliding
as the cord cuts into the palm,
    maybe there's nothing, that's part of it too;
sometimes nothing's all there is. On those days
sweat and stagnant water stink lingers on the ride home.
Nothing's quiet as church, uncomfortable as tight shoes

Julie's come over, gloves on, bucket in hand, arcing against
a sudden gust, her skin bright as copper on ash
Pop's positioned on the ledge
looking into the unseeable, turns back smiling,
so I lock my legs, pull with all I got knowing
we'll make do with whatever's given to us.

What We Are (Father to Daughter)

You see dat stream, Waikahalulu?
Small kid time, we cut school
go play in dat stream,
we make raft, we play pirate, play
plum fight—our clothes get all purple stain.
Huuuuuuuu—Grandma give me dirty lickens when
I come home, but good fun you know.
No can play in Waikahalulu now,
dirty da water see? Everything change,
no mo da same trees
tamarind, kumquat, mountain apple all gone.
We used to fly kite up Punchbowl
by da Filipino camp,
da wind so strong lift you off da ground.
You no see kids fly kite today
everybody forget how fo fly.
I taught you how find rosy apple in da mountain yeah?
Gotta look at da leaf real close,
look like one star. And how fo trap ʻōpae
between da rocks. Lilikoi, guava—
you can tell when ripe
you remember yeah?

Education

A story my Pop loved to tell me:

This professor came to Hawai'i one time, real smart guy. He went
Harvard or Yale or someplace like that, you know, real smart. He was
staying in Waikīkī and went to Coco's, where my Aunty Clara
waitressed. I saw a black-and-white of her one time, Aunty Clara,
tiptoeing on wooden stairs, bare feet, with a button-down short sleeve
tied tight above her waist. She was curvy like the road going up
Tantalus, big eyes and dark wavy hair; guys followed her all ova the
place. Until my Uncle Paul that is: boxing champion, connected, and
kinda nuts about any guy talking to Clara. Well, this professor no can
catch hint my aunty not interested. He keep trying and trying and
trying until Uncle Paul and Pop walks in, sees what's going on. They
sit in a booth across the restaurant, order coffee and watch this guy
make ass outta himself. Clara all worried, so she go hide in the
kitchen. Pop was maybe fifteen, sixteen at the time and he was scared
too, but Uncle, he just drink his coffee like nothing. He says, *What
you worried about kid?* He laughs, orders eggs, and opens the
newspaper. After awhile, Clara's still in the kitchen, so the Prof pays
his check and leaves. Uncle puts down the newspaper, *No let nobody
take what's yours Philip, you understand?* He looks Pop straight in the
eyes, *People, no matta how rich, or how smart, is just animals. When
it's easy to take, dey keep taking. And each time da take gets bigger. You
draw a line around yourself and your family. If anybody come close to dat
line, you fucken step down hard, and you make sure everybody can see,
you hear me?* Then he goes back to reading the newspaper, all calm,
smiling. Later that night, a couple of Uncle's boys went to the Prof's
room to teach the Teach. Nothing serious, just one black eye and one
broken arm. The Prof neva went back to Coco's. Heard he caught the
next plane outta here, a little bit smarter.

He Doesn't Say It with Words, But

It is night. The jalousied window is closed
and the room is dim, illuminated only by
a frosted square lamp on a small wicker table.
The youngest is sick, feverish,
laid out on the thin cushioned floral couch,
cheeks flushed with heat. Her skinny body limp
under well worn Scooby Doo pajamas.
His back is to you, navy blue workpants still on,
the white undershirt untucked.
He is genuflecting, placing a wet dishcloth
over her forehead, his bowed in prayer,
like Jesus in the wilderness asking for strength.
You know he has been doing this all night
walking back and forth across
the cold linoleum floor to rewet the dishcloth,
rinsing out the heat in the kitchen sink
and that he hasn't eaten dinner yet. He will not.
You imagine him bargaining in his prayer, what he'll do
if the fever will just break, just make her well.
You know his next move will be to pull up the flannel blanket
she's kicked off; that she will flutter open her eyes—
You know this is the moment, this is when she knew.

Tea Picking

Fo ti tieng is a Chinese herb thought to promote longevity and prevent aging.

We laughed easily while
picking fo ti tieng which grew wild
in the lawn fronting the Makiki Pumping Station.
Papa and I would start in the shade, our eyes adjusting
to patches of light differentiating green against green.
Immersed between the high blades of grass were
the familiar heart-shaped petals with skinny stems,
tipping themselves towards our fingers.
We carried on, hunched over, inch by inch
filling our market bags as pink powder puffs
from nearby monkey pod trees drifted
across the lawn, content.

At home Papa scattered the fo ti tieng
onto wire nets in the kitchen for drying.
I took more care
placing each stem deliberately,
hearts facing each other in affection

out of that quiet, shriveled small bones—
four nets yielding one handful of tea.
Papa hummed as he opened the cupboard
housing the silver pot with long black handle.
He whispered, *This tea will make you live forever—*
the invisible ever present,
linking the hot coil to the bubbling water
transforming the tea: what was there to question?
He lifted me into his arms, leaned us over
the steam rising, the giving bones,
and I clung to his neck
believing him absolutely.

Last Visit

for my Aunt Rose

Papa rushes in
straightening his shirt
shifting uncomfortably
as he bends over
the bedside.
Her rasping breaths
meter out droplets that
condense, cling to,
slide down
a plastic face mask
clumsily fitted over a
toothless grimace.
Withered limbs contrast
a summer yellow dress
with tulips across the chest—
frivolous attempt
decorating despair
inadequate like Papa's
last minute charity; penance
for thirty years of distance.

Leaving Paradise

Unusual for her to care, but the slight shake
of her shoulders was a tell, twelve is a difficult age.
Somehow, somewhere it began to matter:
the jacket a hand-me-down from her brother
and the rubber bands from yesterday's newspaper
holding back her hair suddenly are awkward,
shameful. Especially on this sunny day
at the waterpark, her first boy-girl party. She decides
to keep her T-shirt on, the ill-fitting blue one-piece
her secret. But the gift wrapped in tinfoil
is not so easily concealed; a solution to the limited
cash in her mother's worn wallet,
It's just like real wrapping paper, it'll be fine.
And the bow, sentimentally put aside at Christmas
now cycling back practical, did help:
the matte yellow contrast against the metallic shine
gave her the courage to come this far—from the car
to the entrance to the gift table set up under the partial shade
of a kukui nut tree. Presents dressed up as flowers,
pink proteas, purple orchids, yellow lehua gathered there
singing out loud. The sun was the first and merciless,
drawing attention to its silvery shell encouraging
the boys' stare, then turned shoulders whispering,
the birthday girl's look of confusion, and another mother's
cover-up, *how clever! how pretty!* She raised a slim smile
for the kindness, and turned from the table
stepping out of Eden.

Poi

Every night Mama would say, *No talk stink—the poi going get rotten.*
So I held my tongue about Sister, Papa stopped talking about the
job, and we ate. Dinners started quiet but ended with laughter; her
admonition clearing away the day. Then came the shortage: taro and
construction. Dinners became moody. I went to college and learned
about the recession. I ate instant potatoes by myself, letting the dishes
pile up till the smell drove my roommate out. I didn't call home. I was
rotten. Once I craved poi, but the market only had day-old, too sour
to hold down.

Divisions

My aunt was far more sophisticated than my mother—
pancake makeup, Cleopatra eyeliner, and her teeth
shiny and straight, even though she chain-smoked Newports.
Uncle had a portrait of her painted and hung
in their dining room; she is seated, draped in cobalt blue
like a Victorian woman of wealth. God loved her—
she was a real live Cinderella sprung from Tin-Can Alley
and made it to the Promised Land, Kahala. We rarely visited
uncomfortable in places with portraits and dining rooms,
so it mattered the times she cupped my face in her hands
and called me pretty. It's easy to remember
her slender shoulders pulling up with her laugh,
her chignon thick and sleek, harder to forget
the gravelly voice calling out to me from room 422
where I worked the night shift on the oncology unit.
She tried to reach us, but we changed our number years ago,
caught me up on how they lost the repair shop—people don't get
their TVs fixed anymore—sold their Kahala home and moved
into a reasonable two-bedroom, easier to clean really
since Uncle can't help too much around the house,
and then of course the cancer. I cupped her face in my hands
and lied. I had to get back to work, yet I took
the stairs skipping steps two at a time down the four flights
till I reached the parking lot to call my sister, who moved
to the mainland ten years ago when construction crapped out.
It was imperative right then that I hear
how each of my nephews was doing in school
I needed to tell her that mom was enjoying Zumba class
and I couldn't breathe until I lifted her
new part-time job at Lowe's, up to the gods.

Fishing at the Hula Show: Kūpuna Division

The slack in their posture
like a palm tree puts you at ease
scarlet hibiscus to match their style
weathered arms pinch and pull
muʻumuʻu up to knees revealing
slips that proper women once wore

so kolohe, stories kūpuna can tell

each with hair dyed to match
what they remember to be true
Auntie Linda's is chestnut
a shade darker than her eyes

she leans forward lightly
coaxing attention with music
in her fingers, looks through
a make-believe peephole
casts a wink

across the room, Uncle Mitch
tips forward with menpachi eyes
lips parted, inhales the flash smile
anticipates the smooth spin

remembers nights at Jubilee's
when he courted her—dancing
to a Kalihi juke band, dangerously
exploring curves. Those same hips
still fluid, hands still able to reel him in.

Tutu's Garden

It seems it's always Sunday,
Sunday when we go to Tutu's
to help clean the garden, all kapakahi
since Tutukane died.

The bamboo patch he planted towards
the back; once slender and elegant like
how Tutu used to look in old black-and-whites,
now so thick, my rusted clippers don't make a difference.
Overripe papayas break under mynah bird beaks
while torch ginger with heavy flower heads
bend like skinny dogs in the wind.

It's so hot over here
even in the late afternoon, I have to
put down this shovel. I try to remember
what the garden looked like
when I was just a kid

there wasn't any heliconia or this
bird of paradise, *too much rubbish*
Tutukane would say, but there was always
a patch of vegetables. Eggplant, squash
and Hawaiian chili peppers to make dinner

You going get cracks you touch dat,
Tutu would yell from da back screen door,
but Tutukane never minded my sister and me
taking a couple cherry tomatoes ripened
by the Waimanalo sun, juice running down
our lips while we plucked handfuls
of yellow ginger for our hair.

Talisman

When they were in love
the days were long, but
the nights were music, big music—
rows of black jackets with brass horns
handled by long lean fingers
pressing furious on ivories,
rolling on drums.
Big band precision and jazz chords jolt
the swell before the refrain,
tension in the strings and percussion
growing larger, larger
sweeping her up and away
from the bakery and the day-old cherry Danish
she tended, away from the shipyard where
he moved pallets
from one warehouse to the next—
a tsunami in that swell's reach that tore
through to that piercing trumpet blast.
It was the rush of being young
the thrill of slow kisses
and late night car rides in a borrowed
green Chevy, with the music
pouring out of the radio,
out over the dark
like it could protect them,
like it could hold back the future.

Mango Season: Another Love Story

She feigns interest as they pass beneath them on the two-mile walk home in the
same gray light they walked to get here. Yes, she's thankful for the extra hours

at work, but she's tired, and would rather not talk. It's his area of expertise anyway:
mangoes. He romanced those trees when he was a boy, swinging his young body

over thick branches, picking burlap bags full of ready red-orange fruit.
Turned them over in Chinatown for quick coins which meant kung fu flicks

and new Converse high-tops. Mangoes have been good to him. He wants her to learn
their names (*See? This one is Pirie, that one is Hayden.*) tell them apart by their leaves,

understand which are best green. She's content with knowing only two kinds:
the ones that have fallen, and the ones out of reach. Her eyes are down, surveying

the bruised, and yellowing; she gathers up the ones not yet under siege by ants.
His eyes are up in the branches calculating each foothold, pointing out

the easy prize right there, just over their heads: but it's late, already so little light.
He closes his fingers around her shoulder like a bowl of loss, and with gratitude

she folds his reluctance into her palms
and holds on.

The Walls of Jericho 1978

The city and all that is in it shall be devoted to the
Lord for destruction.

Joshua 6:17

There is nothing left to offer
except a linoleum floor, thin rug
and 40-watt light bulb.
You flutter and smile little bug,
as if this is enough.

Look at your wellspring
my cracked palms, my swollen feet,
my unnoticeable short hair:
as necessary as the air
and as easily dismissed.

The night shift is tiring little bug
but you want; your father is gone
but you need. With your curls
and stuffed bear, you point and say please—
but the rent is due, and the rent is due.

Each child's cry is a trumpet blast
tearing down these walls
a new city built on the back of this
broken one. In the rubble are
thrift store clothes, a small warm light
and dust.

So tell me of being a ballerina,
a cat doctor, a chef who makes purple-berried
tarts. I live there now as I carry you
in the wrinkle of my eye.
With each breath I will level mountains
for you, so you can fly to places
I will never see.

Laundry 2

She likes to do laundry in the early morning
it's peaceful:
ease of the coin-slide and reassuring clink
the quarters make that starts the water flow.
Even the raggedy outdated *People* magazine
offers up tranquility. Looking at her now,
shock of white hair, still clear eyes, furrowed brows—
she appears to me as she always has,
a citadel without a door and few windows.
I want to ask her how she does it, stays.
Gone are the children who need her protection,
gone is the man who did the damage.
In his place, an old paper tiger.
She could walk away, leave the detergent
and roll of quarters on the folding table and go.
I want to whisper to her there is more
than acceptance, more than the worn treads of old insults.
There are yellow taxis, statues of war heroes,
and piers with fresh fish. I want to put all of it
in her old but still able hands.
There are echoes; *loss, loss, loss* in the plain talk between
mother and daughter, *How are the boys? Stew meat on sale at Safeway*
while the slap of metal zippers hitting the dryer door
manages to startle me with each tumble
even though by now I should expect it.

Thrift Store

In a church thrift store, with old wedding china,
shawls, and faded handbags, Micronesian women whose names

I do not know, women wearing long colorful skirts rummage
through piles of T-shirts three for a dollar, cluck with silver-

capped teeth at their children who hide behind their knees
holding onto plastic toys, *five cents momma, just five cents.*

Shush shush, the mother says as I walk past, nervous smile, nod of the head
past them to the glass case of old costume jewelry looking

for treasures. I walk by their untoned bodies that give birth
and sweep floors and catch buses to thrift stores

open only on Wednesdays and sometimes Saturdays.
I hear their laughter turn to murmurs shuffling through narrow

aisles moving slightly to the side reaching out to their little ones
whose dark eyes widen over the clatter of bent spoons,

the shameful counting out of bus fare then the math—two pants and a pot.
A mother's thankful sigh, *yes yes, you can have it.* Who are they to me

that my hands now seem so small? Their *buzz buzz, coo coo* over
denim and barely bruised shoes in syllables I do not understand.

Coins are passed across the fold-out table to a graying lady with
freckled hands who carefully places the items in plastic bags.

Scurrying feet follow mama past the jingling bell over the door
and into the day, the child's smile dazzling, reflecting

a white light so bright I have to close my eyes against it
as she clutches a one-armed Barbie, heading for home.

Marriage Advice

Old proverbs will tell you marriage
is children and tears. Your aunt
swears lipstick holds it together
and your sister insists Jesus is the answer
but I can only say what I know;
put away everything you think is important
cooking, cleaning, diapering—
those will come like a flood. No need to advance
into that current, marriage will take you there.
What you have to do is learn to build a raft,
something to hold onto when the tides turn.
Build it out of anything you can get your hands on
compliments, sturdy shoulders, tomorrow—those will
do when you are young. You can weather many storms
with those, but when your raft springs a leak:
he loses his job, your back gives out,
and you start drifting down, you will have to build another
with whatever there is; it might be
quiet, magazines, or forgetting. It might have to be lies—
those can last for awhile. The strongest one I built
was made out of television and forgiveness.
I thought it would last forever.
Even at my age, we build or drown.
You want this to work? You want happily ever after?
Then remember girl, marriage is labor
and we get through it tougher. Not shinier.

Westside Dream

You'll be brave when you hear the cops knock,
you'll see a shift in his eyes. You'll want

to slide a slap across his face for the ones you took;
prove something to that nosy bitch watching from across the hall.

Listen. Nobody gives a shit about you,
about him neither when he's pleading his case,

I told you she was crazy, she crazy. Steady yourself.
Remember Leila with the fake tits, fake weave,

and homemade tat across her neck, *Sugar*? If he goes,
he'll call her for bail, you know it. Pull down your shirt. You don't want

to lose him over something like this. When the cops separate you,
smooth your hair, wipe your nose. Think about that kid growing inside you,

think about your sister calling you a whore, think about how good he'll be
when they leave after they remind you two, three times that he'll do it again.

He'll hold you real close, *I'm so sorry baby, I don't know what got into me.*
He'll stroke the hair off your forehead real slow

kiss you gentle over your right eye. *Anything you want baby, anything.*
You'll say cigarettes, and just like that

he's grabbing the car keys and leaving a smile at the door. All's quiet—
only the hum of the plastic fan in the bedroom pushing on. You'll set straight

the green chair and kitchen rags that fell to the floor. You'll reach
for the faucet to get a drink of water and hear your heartbeat.

You'll mistake it for your kid's, you'll mistake it for peace. You'll rub
your belly like they do in the movies and smile thinking it could be.

What the Cops Catalogued

One medium-sized black backpack, frayed edges, missing front zipper; one small vinyl covered New Testament Bible in plastic wrap; one glass pipe shaped in the letters "l o v e"; one pack of cigarettes containing 2 cigarettes; an extra large white tee shirt with surf design—holes at the collar and at the edges; a purple hand towel; 3 small Ziploc bags—empty; 1 medium-sized Ziploc bag containing a bar of soap; a blue Velcro wallet containing 1 ten-dollar bill, 2 one-dollar bills, 2 quarters, an expired bus pass, and a graduation photo of a female; a black plastic digital Casio watch with broken strap; a bent spiral notebook; a black Maglite flashlight and an unopened Snickers candy bar

What my brother told me:

My life is in dat bag Chris, my life.

Shelter

It's not dinnertime yet so you wait
behind the yellow line, the one that stops you
about six feet away from the locked glass window
like at the movies or prison.
The dog-faced chick sitting behind the window,
droopy eyes and double chin ain't looking at you,
ain't giving you the OK to cross over and come up to the window;
state your case about why you should get to go inside.
Doors open at five, and Dog Face will tell you that unless
you have an appointment with a case manager to help
get your shit together, you can't get inside until five.
So you wait, stare down at the yellow line
look back, there's a few more:
an alki in a torn D.A.R.E. tee shirt crouching down,
a haole with dreads, no slippers, laughing to himself, and
a Korean kid, maybe twenty, enveloped in an army jacket
looking straight ahead. All broken in different ways
getting smaller by the minute as cold January cuts through.
No roof over the yellow line to block the drizzle
no walls to shield the wind, just old leaves scraping against
the concrete making a sound
that you remember when you were a boy
playing freeze tag in the open lot next to your house with your sisters.
The memory catches you off guard, *Jesus Christ*—
here's nothing like what you remember:
picking 'opihi, polishing the Nova, Charlotte sober.
You blink back the tears;
memories are whores with sharp teeth.
Papa's voice in your head, *this world ain't for pussies*
something you had to learn on your own
because at the end of nothing
and at the beginning of this line

is where you're standing,
and you got to believe you're worth something,
standing, holding on—even as Dog Face looks through you
and the clock above her head reads 1:15.

Raising Lazarus

Because you were born a boy at a time when having a son meant something

Because you had strawberry blonde hair, played G.I. Joe in the Japanese maple bush fronting the apartment, and didn't cry much

Because you were the only one who would eat ʻopihi with Mom

Because you took the heat for her when Papa came back from the bar

Because you started hanging out with those punks who told you to steal Nana's coin collection

Because he threw you out after you forged checks and tried to cash them at Mom's workplace

Because you shamed the family name in the newspaper

Because your GED meant you could join the Army

Because the Army didn't make a difference

Because you found sanctuary in a pipe and cardboard box

Because she was an addict, too, she took the deal

Because in jail you met Jesus

Because time passes

Because you are his only son

    Papa said, *Come home*

Preparing for the Prodigal Son

Neva even get chance
fo put down da shopping bags
Bradda going come back live here.
I stop in da doorway, screen wide open
When?
He get out next week.
So what, we gotta start hiding all our stuff again?
Da words too sharp too fast.

Papa looks at me out da side
of his eyes, presses his lips together and
breathes real hard through his nose.
Den he looks back down.
For a long time, we no say nothing.

Den, so soft, he says, *Family is family*
I see Papa now, fo da first time,
sitting on dat old kitchen stool,
hands folded between his knees.

I neva know he had gray hair,
gray all ova where da pomade
no can hide. Gray eyelashes, gray
eyebrows. Da bags unda his eyes
dark and swollen, and his brown skin,
so loose now, at his arms and cheeks.

A gecko crawls across da kitchen window.
He lost his tail someplace, but keeps going.

The Man Who Made You Breakfast

The grill is cold; the grease trap is clean enough. He pulls off his hair net, which makes him look more Puerto Rican than Hawaiian, a look he takes pride in. He hangs his apron on the baker's rack before he makes one last sweep of the floor. The familiar scraping of hard blue bristles against tile marks the end of his day. Crumbs and crushed mushrooms are swept out the back screen door while he surveys the parking lot. Pulls back his lips for a slow whistle through battered teeth. He holds up his head now, not like when he first got out. He pretends without fear—no one's gonna remember. He's just another guy working the grill. More than he could hope for. He opens on the weekends and closes on Tuesday and Wednesday nights. He orders the salad dressing and burger buns and reports to the manager on how the specials are moving. For what it's worth, he tells the boss to hire old addicts who are mid-sober over college kids. Terra firma—easier to control. Like him, they know this might be all there is, and the deal isn't so bad: medical plus leftover meatloaf to take home at night. College kids got too much tomorrow to really know how to work. He keeps silent tabs on everyone—the waitresses and their boyfriends, the janitors who get high on their breaks, and even you, how you take your coffee: a survival habit. It's like the inventory he keeps track of, what's coming in and what's going out. He's learned the price of things, and everything has a price.

Loud As Their Love

Empress Restaurant, Chinese Cultural Plaza, banquet room—
the bride was luscious in white lace and rhinestones that
framed her family name in bold letters across her back,
while the groom, daring to wear cornrows and a purple
Samoan print shirt, same print as the bridesmaids' dresses,
all ten of them, signified celebration. Coolers being hustled
table to table—red coolers for guava juice and Diet Coke,
blue coolers for Heinekens—foundations of any good party—
and the ice, like children, was unlimited.
Of course the girls (cinnamon lip gloss, silver hoops)
displayed behind the reception table, disinterestedly sliding
envelopes into the lau hala box, abandoned ship
once the initial rush was over. They glided with importance
endlessly sighing, as not-too-old uncles paid them proper attention.
Both sets of parents were honored with maile, served first,
and joined by the pastor who nursed a green bottle all night.
The DJ gave more shout-outs than necessary,
waiters all equally annoyed while bringing food out
and hauling empty trays back, aunties clinked glasses
whenever Madonna was spun, and the night's shining star,
the couple's daughter, in a miniature matching wedding dress
nestled next to the speakers for a quick nap. After the Mongolian beef
but before the almond float, the bride set out for the money dance
with every *chee-hoo* possible, slapping tables, stomping heels,
dollar bills raining down like manna from heaven, loud as their love.
And we loved them back in that moment:
the groom slipping his arm around her waist, the kiss to the back of
    her neck
her overdone giggle. We loved the flat-chested bridesmaids
    choreographed slick
for a group toast, and the groomsmen huddled together tongue-tied.
    We loved

48

the girls in gold bangles grooving in a circle, daring the boys to join in.
We rejoiced in the red Solo cup! We praised all the unclean and unquiet!
We blessed this union with our mouths full, we blessed the running
    children
with our hands over the tops of their heads, we blessed each other
with smiles and nods and we blessed the night,
which mercifully chose not to loose us too early
to the concrete coming of day.

Waiting: 9 PM Kam Shopping Center

After pacing for fifteen minutes in front of Kenny's Diner,
being simultaneously watched and ignored
by two thick chicks profiled in the window
and the Micronesian security guard sneaking a cig,
I almost decide to leave.
My hand is wrapped tight around the five bills
I agreed to loan you, since you can't
make rent, again, and you brought up the boy
and how he's learning to crawl.
I scan the stores looking for you—
the same old raggedy Baskin Robbins,
run down Payless Shoe Store—nothing changes.
Not the people, mostly Filipinas carrying
their kids and white plastic bags, hustling
to the bus stop. Not the smell,
a mix of sweet sour sauce and diesel.
Not even me, still out of place
waiting on you and swearing to God
this will be the last time.

Why Have Kids

She called today; she's about two months and might be losing the baby. I know her, know her whole world, so I didn't jump when I heard her voice crack after three sentences: *Why?* I tried to be gentle. *It's hard on the body Titi, pregnant in your forties, that's for celebrities with maids and chauffeurs, that's not us. Maybe it's nature's way of letting go, maybe it isn't right.* I hated that word coming out of my mouth: *right*; it felt dry on my tongue, the texture of cheap white bread. It was a cold thing like a featherless baby bird on the sidewalk. I should have used a word with more anchor, a word that could take a hit. Like 'survive' maybe, or 'church' or 'rent.' Those are real things.

    Good. He says when I run into him in the parking lot later in the day. This was before he caught my quiet, before the obvious: *I'll be sixty-five and still working at that shit hole when Michael graduates high school, I'm too damn old for another.* He is. *We're barely scraping by now.* They are. So why did I want to argue with him? *Blind* like the dumb who defend love, or *righteous* like a Born-Again, but it wasn't either. *It could happen* was what I wanted him to know. You hear about it all the time, someone loses their job then wins the lottery, grandmothers wake up with their cancers cured, the scrawny kid grows up to be the quarterback. Things change. When you least expect it, maybe another kid; but it doesn't have to mean pain. What I wanted to say was, *maybe this one will do what we couldn't,* but I kept my mouth shut. I moved to the side, as he got into his rusted-through-blue Corolla, stood there as he sat without moving to put the key in the ignition.

Chevelle

He has never been happy, but with age, he accepts it. The ceiling fan
in the apartment pushes around heat in the summer: balcony view
of a clothesline of another apartment in the next four-story walk-up.
This is his kingdom. Crowded with medical supplies, sagging
furniture, and old friends to keep him safe: Alfred Hitchcock, and
the Creature from the Black Lagoon. He keeps the door locked with
two extra dead bolts and fastens the front jalousies shut. Beyond these
walls, a mere hundred feet shuffle away, his legacy, a 1971 baby-blue
Chevelle. He wants to imagine himself a young man in it: shining
chrome and pinstripe detail, cruising downtown when he had respect,
when women would smile at him, when men would call his name
from a block away and walk over to shake his hand. Wants to imagine
himself without the wife time has also made him come to accept,
without the disappointment of children they had. This is the wrong
time though, a dangerous time for imagining. Once a day he removes
the car cover, and wipes down the hood, the doors and the trunk with
a wet chamois then empties the bucket of water into the street. He
calls out to his wife to help him cover the car back up, sees her lips
moving but can't hear a word. Doesn't matter. He knows that
tomorrow they will go to the supermarket to get papayas and pork
chops. He knows the cancer is not gone no matter what the doctor
says. He knows the thorny familiar things that get him through the
day, sound of worn carpet under feet, sticky skin, and paper plates.
He knows an old man with cancer is a liability, and there was no
better time than before.

Immaterial

I need another after Christmas sale—
brightly lit stores still festooned with green-glitter garland
the thrill of sequins originally $79.99
now just 12 bucks, Korean women calling out
like lunch truck workers over jumbled racks
casting up tangerine blouses for group approval
and mothers speeding through aisles
with aerodynamic strollers.
I need a few open chairs at the food court
Jamba Juice blenders lined up proud as Marines
and the orange chicken from Panda's glazed like a Fabergé egg.
More than anything, I need those faux suede boots, blue,
last pair in the window. Those would be for
Seattle, Portland, or maybe New York
Me, in the boots
sitting indoors, glass from floor to ceiling as I tip
a dark roast to my lips, oversee
the slow drift of snowflakes, *there*.

Here
is a dim hallway from the front door
to your recliner through the kitchen with loose cupboards
and peeling paint, where I have learned to let my ears be my guide;
your breathing can tell me pain or tell me you are asleep.
Here is exactly 27 bottles of medicine kept in a plastic bin
on the bed you no longer sleep in.
I dole them out, the blue, pink, and oblong ones,
morning and night since Mom left. Dove soap pairs
with old washcloths for your fragile skin,
your withered pride while undressing, penance for us both.
Here hope is a wolf but your occasional laugh invites its stay.
We turn off religious talk shows and don't talk about

what is to come. LPs transport you
someplace else, there maybe, but I know
without those boots,
I'll never get to leave.

Odyssey: Midpoint

Untethered yet unable to drown,
we spend your days adrift.
I thought I could predict the waves,
control the tide, but was quickly
brought to my knees, learning
only the edges of your ship's deck
weathered by time and angry gods.
I wanted to be the lookout for your
final journey, Papa,
I wanted to cipher the winds
and arrogantly point out passing curiosities
I know now are invisible to me.
I didn't want monsters for you,
I didn't want the rolling froth
of hospitals, tubes, radiation, legions of white coats
coming at you, fingers pointing at you,
yet there yet there yet there,
and the Sirens call of hope—
Mexico has a cure, Ohio has a cure—
set firmly in your brain, madness and fear,
assuring you, you can stay here in this world.
I thought my presence alone
could shield you Papa,
that you could take shelter in my shadow
but it seems it is always noon.
Even the winds—dear God—a small mercy
against this stifling August heat
has left us.
Pushed on by waves of chemo,
I spend my time untying the knots of our past, still,
casting no shade.

Lost Lessons

After the *Bonanza* reruns were exhausted,
we settled on the Discovery Channel, watching
spinning formless creatures somewhere deep
on the ocean floor, with their black eyes
and open mouths, thriving, unknown to the sun.
The darkness did not envelope, rather,
it suspended the beasts as they wandered
with the ease of angels fanning themselves
against the sand. They sang old songs
in an old language. I remembered you tried
to teach me those songs,
tried to plant them in the darkest, safest
part of my heart; the notes sounded like
Primo beer and empty apartments,
the chords cut like cold linoleum floors
thrummed like a '68 Mustang.
It is a difficult music.
The blue glow of the screen settled
in the valleys of your face, finally,
I tucked you in.

I dreamed of you there with them last night,
swimming in lazy figure-eights—
woke up with a fading tune in my head,
fumbling in the light.

To the End

Weeds quickly overran the tomato patch
and the sectioned-off area for sweet potatoes,
tall useless stalks and thorny burrs choking
the harvest in my square box garden. The futility
in pulling stems close to the roots—
who can bridle spores? or direct the wind?
There is hubris in this,
trying to harness wild things.
In your last moments of light
I insisted you bend to white coats
and codes that spat out your blood analysis,
too much of this, too little of that
eat a spoonful more, sit a little longer, just be
what you never were: submissive.
Instead, you called the doctors assholes
and proclaimed chemo bullshit. You said, *fuck it*
more than once to orders and restrictions, uncivilized
as the deviant sturdy stems that hold their ground
against me. My arrogance in the papers I signed,
the pills I counted out, the way I explained it to you
as gospel; but you didn't need church.
You needed me to throw stones with you,
to walk alongside you to the muddy edge
your life threaded through your own jaw
and bear witness as you clamped down.
How alive you were as the cancer closed in!
How terrified I was—

Upon Your Return

In the last hours of your life,
you were a house on fire
burning down to the foundation
and I was trapped inside

there was no saving you,
just surviving you
and to live through the afterwards.

Now you've returned,
a river flowing over rocks,
effortless under the sky
gently inviting me to listen
to stories you never got to tell:
of the unguarded fence, of red-berried summers.
Listen and forgive you say
to the fragile mistakes of the heart.
Remember how bright you are.

Here's a Poem for You, Bukowski

You might have liked him,
watched him at least,
appreciated the way he said, *sure*
the cool lowering of his eyelids, nod of his head,
cigarette dangling from his lower lip
slow, smooth, *sure*
a man's man

you would have watched her too,
a honey of a wife
when she took out the garbage late at night,
cheap gold chain firm against her breasts

watched her take deep breaths and linger
around the roach infested rusty cans near the street,
no cars rolling through that late at night.
She'd stare down it though
stare for a good minute like she was waiting for something.
You ever saw a woman stare without hope, Bukowski?
without anger, without fear? Like watching a horse race
knowing from the second the gates open, the bet you placed is lost?

When she gets back,
the noises from their apartment,
the crashing of pots, slap of skin, muffled cry—
keep the same rhythm as the moths dancing downstairs
in the liquor store lights.

I don't think you would have taken sides.
I think you would have gotten out of Dodge
and gone to the nearest bar, got a drink, and got laid
in that order. Imagined doing that wife
and not looking in her eyes.
I think you might have been able to relate.

Mercy

According to the guards, he was alone fifteen minutes max before they cut him down; a bed sheet tied to the sprinkler system. That's why his voice was like grated ginger, why I had to bend over to hear him. I hesitated putting my cheek a few inches from his, it wouldn't be the first time a patient spit on me, but we needed some history before going to CT. Defeated homemade tats marked his thin limbs, concave stomach and protruding pelvic bones. He exhaled out the *h*, and I finished the *iv*. He pressed a smile for our collaboration; his openness clearly to protect me. Humbled, I hovered, grabbing the open pack of gauze to dab the tears puddling between his eyes and the bridge of his nose. Those eyes were black like a shark's but soft as a dove's—a splintered view. *I cannot go back.* My hands hesitate. I lose words so I gesture to the guard to take off the shackles; metal's not allowed in the scanner. The guard moves with the speed of a man making overtime. While he jangles back to the other side of the trauma bay, I regroup and take special care to explain what is going on, that the test won't hurt. *Please just stop, please let me die.* Places his faith in my empty hands. *I'm sorry*, and the fluorescent lights overhead color me yellow. Pushing the gurney to the imaging department, we grow miles apart from everyone else and I feel myself becoming as invisible as he is. I take off my glove and stroke his forehead, certain God doesn't remember all of our names.

Believer

She wore her crazy clean, her clothes
were neat, and shoes matched
but the plastic hibiscus pinned over her ears,
purple on the left, fuchsia on the right, gave it away.
She'd come as soon as visiting hours allowed,
packing a pink Thermos bottle filled
with virgin olive oil blessed by the Pope.
She would start by anointing his hands,
reaching over the bed rails on tiptoe
making the sign of the cross on his forehead
and finally grazing his thighs above
the knees, calves, and feet amputated a week ago.
Fearless the way she touched the gauze
covering his wounds, sacred how she said his name—
Gino—said it slow like a first kiss,
protective as a priest. She told him to be strong,
and that it was a sure thing about getting the apartment,
so he had to get better to help decorate;
reassured him his legs would grow back.
I said nothing. Sniffing once, like a coyote does
she caught a scent: my disbelief, my sickness.
All things are possible through Him, amen, amen.
Doubling-down on the word and gripping Gino's hand,
it was damnation for those afflicted
with the fungus of acceptance
of this world, of these murky waters
holding us together: patients, families, nurses, doctors
even those alone, like her, half in smoke, half in ashes,
keeping eyes closed, refusing to see.

Transplant

I never thought of you out there,
patrolling that well-bred neighborhood beyond
the mall and complaints of wrinkled women,
ugliness everywhere. This city does not
belong to us; we cannot make it ours.

I keep to the lighted side of the street
less addicts and anger there,
as I scurry back to a Homewood Suites,
waiting for your shift to be over.
I listen to the local news:

an old man with bloodied hands and starched shirt
confesses to chopping up his wife,
the still missing two-year-old with green-flecked eyes,
and the CNN headliner: four cops ambushed—
shot in the head at one of your quaint coffee houses.

I meet you for lunch, see you seated
at the counter against a large window of steel
and glass rectangles framing sprigs of cherry blossoms,
soft blue sky—almost perfect.
Over coffee you tell me of the ungodly
paperwork and eating with the other brown cops.
You tell me the women here do not want you,
think you are Mexican. We laugh.
On the flight home, I spend the hours
wondering how you will die.

If I Were an Optimist

the obvious would be to write about this garden
filled with the buzz of bees overhead
in the flowering avocado tree, the creep
of curling pumpkin leaves along the wooden box,
or even of the neighbor cat, wading
through a thicket of red torch ginger
cautious black paw over cautious black paw,
sniffing at broken patches of afternoon light.
You would squint at the obtuse;
the many fallen leaves not yet swept away,
a cracked stone pathway,
shocking burst of purple eggplant.
All of it as proof
that the untended finds its way without us—
they bloom and fall and move in miracles
while we give our hearts away.
Reel in quiet revelation,
the cat leaping up at a white butterfly,
a furtive glance from an ordinary dove,
and the teacup beside me
balanced in the grass
half full.

Old Letter

I was glad to be alone to open the old letter,
prepared, but not really, for the jolt words can bring.
I forgot

my world dwindled since that time:
books, a bed, sound of the wind.
Satisfied with little,
I listen to the rustle of lace curtains

then the crackle of old paper
dashed out script—several lines only
addressed to *Angel* and signed
with love. Darkening

I knew your wife would have erased
me long ago. No stumbling over
old photos or letters for you—
worse than vanished, resolved.

I moved, only because the phone rang,
to the chair, to the window,
to the chair. Put on my blue blouse:
all breath and gravity.

reminded myself of my place

tucked you back into the appropriate shoebox
away from the light where only cruel things
and stars dwell

then after the long hour
the tending-to-night, another day.
Like this sun, I too will go down
faithless, without memory.

Recipe for Grief Tartare

It is essential you start with fresh grief—
old grief can be tough and difficult to chew
no matter how long you marinate it.
Remember to keep grief at room temperature;
if you refrigerate it, you'll get revenge
which is an entirely different dish.
Grief should be handled as little as possible,
no excessive kneading, twisting, or cutting it.
Once you've opened your grief
and allowed it to sit for awhile,
break into small manageable pieces
as grief quickly overwhelms.
A serving size of one is best although it can be shared.
Plate in the dark and do not mix with alcohol (a common mistake)
Garnish you grief generously with salty tears
and swallow whole.

The Architecture of Poems

Of course we all want our poems to be
the Taj Mahal, where each curved window
breathes sex in the almond scented morning,
hundreds of them looking onto a marble courtyard
built around fading stars, cognac-colored stallions, and a god or two.

Every word a gilded room that overflows
mezzo sopranos combing their long black hair, drinking sangria
freshly made with oranges and lime.

The outer corridors—metaphors—darkening echoes
impenetrable to light. Lining the pathway, locked camphor chests filled
with broken wings. Wooden beams holding up the walls carry the names of
all our dead, even our stillborns, of failed cities, and dried-up gardens.

But what about the three-story walk-up poems?
The mundane, square box, beige poems, where
you'll find me laying in the kitchen on a green
braided rug I got on sale at Pier One, holding
an empty Ben & Jerry's carton in one hand,
and a spoon filled with shame in the other.
I am there, staring up at the old black phone,
its stretched-out cord, willing you to call.

The Compromise

I do not have the same things with him
that I had with you, but I have different
things, good things, quiet things

a terracotta-tiled roof and mock orange hedges,
sheets of lined paper and unbrushed hair,
old patchwork quilt, blue seashells,
a bowl of Portuguese bean soup.

I also have a tiger in the basement.
he constantly sniffs at the door
pacing between old age and remembering.
He never blinks
and waits for my shadow
to cross the floor.

Healing

When you left
it was a drier, brighter summer
than I would have liked. Still,
a world.

I sleep uncomfortably
in the heat, in the light, nowhere
to shield myself from the normalness
of things—

a foam cup of lukewarm coffee,
in the sink one dish, one fork,
folded laundry not yet put away.

Time is sturdy here,
facts remain facts
and the beasts of my imagination slowly
retreat to their caves.

I catch myself waiting
for another storm, for the thunder,
for an unexpected hallelujah
that would make me shake
or at least blink
but everything goes on
telling me—*no harm done.*

October Morning

A gray-violet sky softens through thin curtains
while fallen dried mango leaves bristle
and a cool breeze patiently paces outside my window.
Autumn is here—
along with my black cat Mowgli,
claws clicking across the old wood floor.
Effortlessly he leaps, arcs
and lands on Nana's green quilt at my feet,
carefully avoiding the books I've nested in overnight—
twigs of poetry and vampire lore—
as he makes his way to the head of the bed
drapes scarf-like over my neck and purrs
his singular prayer:
Feed Me
These mornings are the quiet harvest,
bounty of the year's heartache;
the fruit of hanging on and dumb luck.
I close my eyes and match my breathing to his
not wanting to jinx it,
this lull before the coming of winter.

Sand Island Revisited

I drive past the rusted tower
    sewage-salt water taints the air
    rubbish weeds litter the view
Was it here?
My uncle's fishing village, my weekend home? No,
not here. Not this tent city, this drug haven, this
attemptable   manicured   park. I drive past

to where parking lot meets grassy field.
Bowed, I step here for the first time in twenty-five years:
Sand Island. I am not here
to fish or pick limu—
those days are gone. I come
to make ipu heke with my brothers and sisters, together
we go over the grassy slope to the sand divide: I see

waves still curve diamonds and sun still burns
my hapahaole skin. Sand still is large and coarse,
not fine like imports at Waikīkī
    we need rough to smooth our ipu
    we need rough to shape our way

Our laughter carries over to Mokauea. Resurrected,
the shore break chants—*we remain we remain we remain*

Acknowledgments

Grateful acknowledgment is made to the following publications in which some of these poems first appeared, some in slightly different forms: *Crab Creek Review* ("Kings"); *Honolulu Stories: Two Centuries of Writing* ("Sand Island," "What We Are," "Sand Island Revisited"); *Hawai'i Review* ("Last Visit," "The Walls of Jericho 1978"); *Blue Collar Review: Journal of Progressive Working Class Literature* ("Divisions," "The Man Who Made You Breakfast"); *Hawai'i Pacific Review: Best of the Decade* ("Fishing at the Hula Show," "Old Letter"); *Haight Ashbury Literary Journal* ("Laundry 2," "Westside Dream," "What the Cops Catalogued").

I would like to thank my parents Evelyn and Philip for giving me not only the things I needed, but instilling in me the desire to do better. Mom—you have shown me that strength comes in many different forms. Pop—you would always say, *Don't tell me what you going do Chris, show me.* I try to, Pop. Don't worry, I'm taking care of Mom and I miss you more than I thought I could.

Special thanks to my husband who always listens to my poetry drafts when I ask for advice, yet doesn't hold it against me when I don't take it. You are my rock.

To Eric and Darrell: Mahalo for not only taking a chance on publishing my work and inviting me into the Bamboo Ridge 'ohana, but for your life's work of making this journal and carving out a place for Hawai'i locals to have a voice. It is not an overstatement to say that the authenticity that surrounds local writing since the first stapled cardstock edition of *Bamboo Ridge* stems from your accomplishments. From your vision, local talent is being picked up and shared in the mainland and beyond. Where would we be as local writers without your work? I won't even think about it. You guys are better than Batman.

Thank you to my teachers Adele Ne Jame and Robert Sullivan, who taught me to love language and all its possibilities—like how it can make us strong in all our weak places. The world needs more teachers like you.

To the Bamboo Ridge Study Group: Wing Tek, Marie, Mavis, Gail, Lisa, Michelle, Juliet, Lee, Jean, Ann, Darrell, Eric, and Joe—each of you have contributed to my growth as a writer and I cannot thank you enough for letting me be a part of this group. I look forward to our meetings knowing that the space that is created by each member's talent and perspective is sacred ground; not many people will experience this kind of openness and true desire for another to succeed. How lucky I am.

A special mahalo to Lisa Linn Kanae, Gail Harada, Juiet Kono Lee, Joy Kobayashi-Cintrón, and Wing Tek Lum, whose tireless efforts and oversight have made this book a reality. I know you have spent countless hours to get the best for me, far beyond what I am aware of, and I am grateful for each of you, will always be.

One more mahalo to Rowen Tabusa and Russell Sunabe whose artwork and skill elevate my work. You've shaped and dressed my humble words into a collection that I feel blessed to dedicate to my father.

And lastly, to the *Renshi* Ladies; these past couple of years have taken me to places and experiences I never would have had without you. Over and over when I look back at what we have done and how close we have become, all I feel is blessed. Juliet—truly, I never would have written this book without your encouragement or imposed deadlines. You are my hero.

Christy Passion is a critical care nurse and poet. Her singular works have appeared in various local journals and anthologies, as well as in mainland and international journals such as *Crab Creek Review*, *Haight Ashbury Literary Journal*, *Blue Collar Review*, and *Mauri Ola*. She has received the James A. Vaughn Award for Poetry, the *Atlanta Review* International Merit Award, and the Academy of American Poetry Award. Her first book, *No Choice but to Follow*, is a collaboration of linked poetry. She works and resides in Honolulu.